Why so many

SOLVING THE CRISIS IN HOMESCHOOLING
Exposing the 7 major blind spots of homeschoolers

(Also published under the title
Solving a Crisis in Christian Parenting)

Reb Bradley

FAMILY MINISTRIES PUBLISHING
Sheridan, California

FAMILY MINISTRIES PUBLISHING
PO Box 266
Sheridan, California 95681
www.familyministries.com
800-545-1729

Booklet version COPYRIGHT © September 2006 by Reb Bradley
Book version COPYRIGHT © March 2013 by Reb Bradley
Printed in the United States

Based on the first session in Reb's CD series "Influencing Children's Hearts." Originally published in Reb's electronic newsletter as a series of articles entitled "Solving the Crisis in Homeschooling."

Table of Contents

Preface   5

Introduction   7

Blind Spot #1: Self-Centered Dreams   10

Blind Spot #2: Family as an Idol   13

Blind Spot #3: Emphasis on Outward Form   18

Blind Spot #4: Tendency to Judge   23

Blind Spot #5: Over-Dependence on Authority and Control   32

Blind Spot #6: Over-Reliance Upon Sheltering   44

Blind Spot #7: Formulaic Parenting Hinders Relationship   76

More help from Reb Bradley   97

Preface

According to research, more Christian young people than ever before are forsaking their childhood faith. In one study conducted by LifeWay Research[1] it was discovered that a whopping 70% of Christian young adults dropped out of church at some point between the ages of 18 and 22.

LifeWay's polling uncovered a variety of causes for such weakness of faith in young people, but most of those reasons will not be discussed here. My purpose in this book is to discuss just one reason that good homeschooled children grow up to turn from the faith their parents sought to give them. Specifically, I will look at how diligent parents accidentally contribute to their children's decision to go wayward. This book is about uncovering parental blind spots and healing broken relationships.

---

[1] "Teenage Dropout Study," LifeWay Research, 2007; http://www.lifeway.com/Article/LifeWay-Research-finds-reasons-18-to-22-year-olds-drop-out-of-church

Introduction

In recent years, I have heard from multitudes of troubled homeschool parents around the country, a good many of whom were leaders. These parents have graduated their first batch of kids, only to discover that their children didn't turn out the way they thought they would. Many of these children were model homeschoolers while growing up, but sometime after their 18th birthday they began to reveal that they didn't hold to their parents' values.

Many of these kids were model children while growing up, but sometime after their 18th birthday they began to reveal that they didn't hold to the faith their parents has sought to give them.

Some of these young people grew up and left home in defiance of their parents. Others got married against their parents' wishes, and still others got involved with drugs, alcohol, and immorality. I have even heard of exemplary young people who became atheists in their first months of college. My own adult children have gone through struggles I never guessed they would have faced.

Most of these parents remain stunned by their children's choices, because they were fully confident their approach to parenting was going to prevent any such rebellion. Some were especially confident, because as younger teens these kids had been respectful and obedient. Needless to say, the dreams of these homeschool parents have crashed, and many younger parents want to know what they can do to prevent their own children from following the same course.

When my three grown children were young, I was overly confident in my approach to parenting. I was convinced that my children would grow up godly, and that they would avoid significant struggles with sin because of my parenting. I was absolutely certain that since I was training them "in the way they should go," and I was doing most everything I had written in my Child Training Tips book, I would be a success as a parent. However, I had yet to discover it wasn't all about ME and MY success. In fact, I had yet to learn that the parents who think it's all about THEIR success are often contributing to their children's struggles. (Revelation #1 – proper parenting is about the *children* not the *parent*. I'll explain in Chapter One.)

As each of my three oldest children reached adulthood I was shocked to discover that they did not conform exactly to the values I had sought to give them. They had retained *much* of what I had given, but not *everything*. Instead of being perfect reflections of my training, they each turned out to be individuals who had their own values and opinions. I had wrongly thought them to be exactly like wet clay, me being the potter with total control over what they would become. I was not prepared for their individuality, nor was I ready to see them as fleshly beings. As I watched them each face off with the Lord and have their own struggles with the flesh, like I had when I was their age, my homeschool dreams crashed royally.

After several years of examining what went wrong in our own home and in the homes of so many conscientious parents, God has opened our eyes to a number of critical blind spots common to homeschoolers and other family-minded people.

Blind Spot #1: Self-Centered Dreams

I have observed that it is easy for conscientious parents to become "dream" oriented. The reason that our dreams for our children are so vulnerable to crashing is because they are *our* dreams, but they involve our *children*. Our dreams are not just for *them*, but also for *us*. As homeschool parents we make great sacrifices and invest a great deal to influence how our children turn out. The problem is that love for children can be lost in love for personal success as a parent. Our concern for ourselves ends up overshadowing our love for our children.

When my oldest son was 18 he developed habits of disrespectful communication and I had to ask him to leave my home for a season. (In Israel the most severe discipline for lawbreakers was execution – next to that, it was *setting someone outside the camp*.) Needless to say, my wife and I were devastated by the discipline we imposed. In the first month he was gone we wept each day for him. We were grieved that he was now unprotected from the junk from which we had worked so hard to shelter him, but more than that, I was heartbroken that my dreams for him and our family would no longer come true. I remember speaking the words to him, *"Son, you've ruined my dreams."* You see, I had a dream for my family and it involved adult children who lived at home humbly under parental authority, and who would one day leave home to marry, after following my carefully orchestrated courtship process. But now, my son had gone and "messed up" my perfect dream.

Nothing is wrong, of course, with dreaming of good things for your children, but the truth was, my dream for my son was mostly about *me*.

In hindsight, what was particularly grievous was that I was more worried about the failure of my dream of "success" than the fact that my son and I had a broken relationship. Although he was restored to us four months later, it still took me years to realize that we had had a damaged relationship and that I had contributed to it. (More on that later.)

All homeschool parents want to accomplish something good in their children. Success in parenting requires that academic, moral, and spiritual goals be set. It is only natural for parents to have high hopes and dreams for their children. However, when we begin to see our children as a reflection or validation of *us*, we become the center of our dreams, and the children become our source of significance. When that happens in our home it affects the way we relate with our children, and subtly breaks down relationship. As relationship breaks down, so does parental influence.

Blind Spot #2
Family as an Idol

We dream for results, but preoccupation with results can turn the family into a measurement of success. For those who feel successful, family becomes a badge of honor or trophy to be admired by others or God. When we allow the success of our family to determine our security or sense of wellbeing we are seeking from it something God intends us to receive from *Him*. I am describing idolatry. If homeschoolers are not careful, family can easily become an idol.

At times in their history the Israelites worshipped idols. They didn't always forsake worship of the living God – they merely served other gods along with Him. Sometimes they simply made an idol of something good. Jesus rebuked the Pharisees because they elevated issues of holiness higher than the very God who declared them holy.[2] An idol is anything other than God in which we seek security and fulfillment. It may be something biblical or good, but if it has the power to determine our

---

[2] Mat 12:1-8; 23:24

wellbeing, we have elevated it higher than God meant for us. As those who are devoted to our families, and therefore invest a great deal of time, energy, and heart, it is easy to elevate the family too high.

We know we have made our family an idol when we put our hope and trust in it more than in God – we look to *it* rather than God for our identity and significance. And we know we look to our family for our significance when it has the most power to lift us up or to demoralize us. It is most obvious in a public setting when we either glory in our children or become enraged when they embarrass us. Our children are either the source of our pride or our disappointment, depending on whether or not they help us achieve our image of a strong family.

A great problem with idolatry is that idols require sacrifice, and we end up sacrificing relationship with our children for the idol of the family. When we elevate the image of the family, we effectively trade our children's hearts for our reputation.

Craving a reputation for success puts great pressure on us, and then on our children – we feel quite constrained to succeed with them. If they turn out okay, then we can credit ourselves with success, but if they struggle or fail, then we may live with guilt, embarrassment, and bitterness towards them. Many dedicated parents look at the choices made by their teen and adult children and live under a cloud of failure or resentment.

In the Christian life it is important to understand that our highest success is not measured by the effect we have upon others, but strictly by our obedience to God. In other words, God does not credit us that someone came to faith in Christ through our words – He credits us for our obedience. We obey and speak the truth – God bears the fruit.[3] Parents, therefore, must do what is right and acquaint their children with Christ and His ways. They must train, discipline and instruct, with the intent, obviously, of bringing maturity and leading their children to Christ. However, from God's standpoint, parents' success is measured by their obedience – not by how their children ultimately choose to respond to their influence.

In 1987, shortly after I planted a church, we were visited by Pastor Richard and Sabina Wurmbrand. (They both had been tortured for years in communist prison camps and are the

---

[3] 1 Cor 3:6

godliest people I have ever known.) During their visit Sabina asked me how the church plant was going. I responded, saying that I believed I was in obedience to God to plant the church, so anticipated that it would be a success. For that statement she firmly rebuked me. She looked me in the eye and declared, "Obedience **is** the highest success!"

Those life-changing words transformed my view of ministry, and impacted my parenting. It is our responsibility to obey the Lord – to sow the seed and to water – it is His job to make the seed grow.[4]

I once believed and taught that a parent could follow the right biblical steps and be guaranteed of raising children who remained faithful to God from childhood into their adult years. In fact, as a parent of young children I judged as a failure any parent whose young adult children were prodigal. However, as my own children aged and I discovered that they were self-determining individuals with their own walks with Christ, I came to the alarming realization that I had a lot of control over their outside, but not their inside. They were like **all**

---

[4] *"I have planted, Apollos watered; but God gave the increase." 1 Corinthians 3:6*

adults who were faced with the choice of whether or not they were going to listen to Christ and follow Him. As Christians we all encounter opportunities many times in our lives – to choose to follow Christ or not. It was a rude awakening for me when I saw that even the best parenting could not exempt an adult child from making the wrong choice when faced with temptation. I do believe that by our influence we can greatly increase the likelihood our children will grow up to love and follow Christ, but I see nothing in Scripture that guarantees well-trained children will never succumb to temptation.

Consider the parable of the Prodigal Son. The righteous father raised two sons who turned out sinful – one went deep into sin and then repented – the other stayed home obediently, yet was polluted with pride and bitterness. Could the Father take blame or the credit for their sinful choices? Not at all, for the story is about God the Father Himself – it is a lesson about His mercy to His children when they fail. May we learn from God's example!

Blind Spot #3
Emphasis on Outward Form

Preoccupation with results often leads to emphasis on outward form. When we are preoccupied with achieving results it is natural to admire the results others seem to have achieved with their children. We like the way the pastor's kids sit reverently in the front pew and take notes of their father's sermon, so we go home and begin to teach our children to sit reverently and to take notes. What we don't know is that the pastor's kids conduct themselves with reverence and attentiveness not because he "cleaned the outside of the cup" and simply drilled them to do so -- he lived a genuine love for Jesus that was contagious, and watched as the fruit was born.[5] Parents are destined for disappointment when they admire fruit in others and seek to emulate merely that *expression* of fruit in their own children. Fruit is born from the inside -- not applied to the outside.

Imagine that the fruit you desired was the edible variety, so you went out into your yard

---

[5] Mat 23:26

and planted an apple tree. Just suppose that one day, while you were waiting for the apples to begin growing on your tree, you caught a glimpse of a neighbor's apple tree. You noticed in admiration that its branches were laden with big, luscious apples. What would you do? Would you run to the produce market to buy some apples, then go home, and in the dead of night, tie them onto your tree? If you did, the sight of your tree might really impress your neighbors. But that is not what you would do. You would likely go to the neighbor and ask how he cared for and fertilized his tree to produce such fruit. It is the same with our children – luscious fruit will be born from what we put into them – not from what we tie onto them. As a matter of fact, in no time, the fruit that we put onto our children will rot and fall off.

In the homeschool community I have observed that there can be a great emphasis on outward appearance, whether it is dressing for excellence, modesty, grooming, respectful manners, music style, or an attitude of sober reverence in worship. Some even take their children down a country path of humble fashions, raising food, and making bread. Nothing is wrong with any of these things, but we must be careful – we can model for our children outward changes and easily fall into molding their *behavior* and/or *appearance*, while missing their *hearts*. In some circles emphasis on the *outward* is epidemic.

(A friend of mine, a homeschool mom, just passed away of cancer. In the week before she died, I asked her if she had any regrets in her life. She told me she wished she had baked less bread – she said if she had it to do over again she would buy bread and spend more time with her children. Even though she had sometimes included the children in her breadmaking, she had invested time and energy in pursuing the "path" because she thought it was part of the spiritual homeschool package.)

Let us not forget that Jesus came against the Pharisees for their preoccupation with what they felt were legitimate expressions of spirituality. They measured holiness by what was avoided and by what would be seen by others.[6] The Pharisees were earnest in their religion, but they were preoccupied with outward expressions of holiness rather than hearts of humility and love[7] that would bear genuine fruit. I find it fascinating that in the

---

[6] Mat 6:1-2, 5, 16; 23:5-6, 23-28; John 7:24
[7] Micah 6:8

gospels there is not one mention of Jesus coming against immodesty, even though among his followers were prostitutes and the like. Jesus emphasized cleaning up the inside while the Pharisees were the ones preoccupied with cleaning up the outside. We must ask ourselves: Which are we more like – Jesus or the Pharisees? Even now do we justify ourselves, insisting we emphasize cleaning up both the inside and the outside?

I know that some react strongly to these assertions, so let me emphasize that I *do* want my wife and daughters to adorn themselves modestly. God did address it once in the New Testament,[8] but we must ask ourselves, is it possible that we have elevated modesty, or other issues of outward form, higher than Jesus did? If he only mentioned modesty once in the epistles and never mentioned it in his earthly ministry, but instead emphasized the importance of a changed heart bearing outward fruit, should we not follow his example and concentrate on reaching our children's hearts? Because He did address it in the first epistle to Timothy, let us teach our children the value of keeping private that

---

[8] 1 Tim 2:9

which should be, but let us be careful of thinking that just because they look moral on the outside that they have God's values on the inside. Concurrently, let us also be careful of measuring everyone else's enlightenment by what we have decided is modest, spiritual, or holy.

Blind Spot #4
Tendency to Judge

One of the side effects of focusing on keeping the outside of the cup clean is that it becomes easy to judge others by our personal standards. You see, in setting standards for our family, each of us must work through a process of evaluation and analysis to decide what is safe, wise, or permissible. Once we become convinced of our personal standards, not uncommonly, it follows that we believe they should apply to others as well.

One of the things that characterized the Pharisees was that they created their own standards of holiness related to outward appearance, and then belittled others who didn't hold to their standards. Jesus spent a lot of time exposing the Pharisees for their shallowness and their self-righteousness judgments, yet, many of us homeschool parents have inadvertently followed the Pharisees' path -- we have overly elevated *outward form* and we have condescended to those who appear less enlightened.

One of the ways that will reveal if, in fact, we have gone the way of the Pharisee, is that when we believe we have achieved results with our children, we become proud of our accomplishments. In our pride, we then judge others by those areas in which we feel most successful.[9] If we would never permit our baby to make a peep in a meeting we will feel distain for any mommy who allows her baby to fuss. If we would never dream of watching TV, we will feel sorry for the pastor and his "lack of enlightenment" if we know he owns a television with satellite hookup. If a child calls us by our first name instead of Mr. or Mrs., we marvel at his parents for his lack of upbringing.

It is a fair assumption that if we make <u>*preeminent*</u> for our families issues of outward appearance (such as humble fashions, modesty, and grooming) we will likely condescend to those who don't hold to our standards. If we are proud of our children's public etiquette and conduct, it will be easy to belittle those who don't measure up. If we condemn everything but our preferred music style, we may avoid all those who hold to a different standard in music. Standards in these areas are subjectively derived and based

---

[9] Luke 18:9

largely on personal opinion, yet if we are convinced *our* opinion is *God's* opinion, we may count those who don't hold to them as being in error or at the very least misguided.

It is easy to miss this area of pride because we may not express our judgments "arrogantly." We may not say something condemning like, *"My goodness, I couldn't believe it when I heard the Smiths say they were putting their oldest children into school next year! They're sacrificing their children for convenience. Seems to me they're either compromising or giving up. I was afraid this would happen when they began attending that new church!"* Instead, we may wrap our judgments in compassionate sounding words, *"I'm so grieved to hear about the Smiths' decision. How far they have fallen -- it's so sad. We'll pray that they see the light again! I hate it when the devil deceives God's people!"* Arrogance wrapped in compassionate tones can be especially deceiving.

(Pride is so deceptive that we won't know our judgments are even *judgments*. We will think we are just making observations and feeling pity, when in fact, we are looking down on others from our lofty place of confident enlightenment. It is a high view of ourselves that allows us to condescend to and belittle others in our mind. And if you already knew all this, be careful – it is our pride that causes us to be amazed that others didn't see what was so obvious to us.)[10]

Typically, when we belittle others who don't measure up to our standards, we will also imagine others are judging us. Consequently, we will find ourselves frequently being defensive. We assume that others will think lowly of us for some perceived inadequacy, so we offer unsolicited explanations and clarifications for us or our children. For example, let's say we walked past a TV at Sears and saw something of interest – when we tell others what we saw, we are careful to clarify that we saw it at Sears and weren't watching a TV at home. When judgment is in our own heart we imagine it is in others. (And when we are among likeminded judges the judgment is not just imagined – it is *real*.)

If we live under fear of judgment, not only will we tend to be on the defensive, but whenever we are in a public setting where our children might be "watched," we will put pressure on them. If that setting is church,

---

[10] For more help with understanding your heart, consider securing yourself a copy of the CD set Motives of the Heart.

preservation of our reputation will require our children always be on their best behavior. If they sit there silently when everyone else is singing a hymn, we look down with intensity and whisper, *"Sing! Show some respect to God."* If they wiggle too much we scrunch up our face, squeeze their leg, and say, *"Sit still!"* If they draw pictures while we see other children listening to the pastor we quietly instruct them, *"Put that away and pay attention."* Obviously, nothing is wrong with wanting our children to respect God, control their bodies, and listen to Bible teaching, but fear of judgment is the wrong motivation. Besides, if we do succeed with molding our children's *outward* behavior to be impressive in public, we will easily condescend to those whose children's behavior is not.

It is important to note that when pride is working its work in us, we sincerely believe our personal opinions reflect God's utmost priorities and standards. We validate ourselves since we know we keep those standards, and by the same standards others are validated or invalidated in our eyes, as well. For example, if we are self-validating, we may decide that since we have chosen to teach our children at home, anyone who won't homeschool doesn't love their children enough to sacrifice for them. If we are self-validating, it means that since we think we understand the true definition of modesty, anyone who doesn't dress according to our standard is carnal, unenlightened, or has fallen away. A self-validating person is justified in their own eyes and in the eyes of those with whom they fellowship.

What we believe to be our "enlightened" perspective becomes a filter by which we gauge others' spirituality, and therefore limits our options for fellowship. We develop a very narrow definition of what we call "likeminded" people, based on the outworkings of our values and opinions. For example, if we think drums are carnal and have no place in worship, we might walk into a church and decide we cannot fellowship there if we spot drums and no organ – the drums completely discredit the church to us. Or a Bible teacher is entirely discredited in our eyes, because he does not use our preferred Bible translation, or prays with what we feel is insufficient sobriety. Or we meet someone and immediately trust their spirituality simply because they educate their children like we do, dress to our standard, and require quick obedience of their children. It is easy for us "family-minded" people to elevate our opinions and personal convictions and make them grounds for fellowship. But are we on a path to exclusivity when we will no longer associate with those who will be with us in eternity? Is it possible we have lost sight of fellowship based on love and devotion to Jesus, and have substituted personal standards and a narrow view of Christian liberty?

There are several serious consequences of raising children in a home marked by pride and judgment. Our example of emphasizing the outward and making critical, judgmental remarks about others will impact our children negatively.

a. They may learn from our example to judge others and grow up with our shallow values. If we don't know that our values are shallow we will regard our children as virtuous and be proud of them. When our children point out to us the parenting mistakes, shortcomings, or spiritual blindness of others, do we correct them for their arrogance or do we affirm them for their "insights"? We mustn't be pleased when our children seek our affirmation by noting the failings of other parents or children – we must direct them into an attitude of compassion and respect.

b. If they do not learn to judge others from our bad example, it may be because they fear our judgments of them. They feel they are just like the ones they hear us judge, so hide their real values from us. We mustn't be surprised if they act like they embrace our values during their teen years, when in fact, they are simply seeking to avoid discipline and lectures. In reality they have closed off their hearts to us and will likely leave home as soon as they get the chance.

c. It is also possible that they see the shallowness of our "religion" and are not attracted to it in the least. Christianity is not a system of do's and don'ts – it is *surrendering to a wonderful Savior who gave his life for his people*. A legalistic faith consisting primarily of "avoid this, wear that, and attend this" is not attractive to most children. Such children grow up full of knowledge and rules, but lack attraction for the Lord Jesus. They may identify themselves with Christ at an early age, but it is possible that the Christianity they learned from us was characterized chiefly by religious rules and doctrines. They will eventually forsake their identification with Christ because they grew up under the weight of religious standards, but lacked the grace and power to carry them out. Many such young people have forsaken "religion," and still need to find Jesus and the grace of salvation.

I want to suggest that this area of pride and judgment is a difficult one to identify and renounce. By its very nature, pride acts as a filter for our thinking and therefore, our perceptions. We feel self-justified. So I pray, even at this moment, that God will open our blind eyes and bring freedom to us all. If we are able to leave a judgmental outlook behind we increase the likelihood of our children finding in us the beauty of our Savior, Jesus.

Blind Spot #5
Over-Dependence on Authority and Control

When we are preoccupied with outward form our focus tends to become shallow and behavior oriented. We look upon our children as if they are roses that can be trained to grow a certain direction by constant pruning and binding. Consequently, we rely heavily upon our authority in an attempt to bring our children under our total control. We assume if we give them the Word of God, shelter them from harmful influences, discipline them consistently, and maintain high standards for their *outside*, that their *inside* will inevitably be shaped.

I recall that when I first started teaching on parenting many years ago, I actually used the illustration of training roses to describe proper rearing of children. I was mistaken to do so – not because it is an incorrect example of training, but because it is an *inadequate* one. To successfully train roses requires a goal, a plan, and diligence in labor. Fruitful training of children requires the same. However, the difference is that roses have no mind of their own and only grow as they are allowed. Children are people – self-determining individuals – and they ultimately choose how they will respond to parental influence.

If we fail to understand this we will be tempted to intensely control our children up into their adult years. We will hold them tightly in the mold of our choice up until the day we release them from the home, thinking that they will maintain the shape of our mold as they venture into their married lives. Sometimes as parents we give ourselves way too much credit for the power we have in our children's lives. Such a perspective insures we will develop a dominating style of parenting that will likely damage our relationship with our teenagers and hinder our ability to truly influence their values.

No amount of parental control or restriction will guarantee that a child will turn out exactly as directed. Obviously, our training increases the *likelihood* our children will cling to the faith when they reach maturity, or turn back to Christ if they do enter a season of rebellion, but our training does not *guarantee* the desired outcome.

I know that some will struggle with the assertion that parents do not have total control over the outcome of their parenting, because of Proverbs 22:6. And I would have struggled too, many years ago, but upon examination of the passage in question, I am convinced that it is a verse meant as an *admonition of wisdom*, not as an *absolute guarantee of outcome*. Like many of the sayings in Proverbs it is written as a statement of *probability* and not as a *promise*.

A literal rendering of the Hebrew of Proverbs 22:6 reads: *"Dedicate a child specifically toward a righteous path of life and he will not abandon it when he reaches old age."* Proverbs is a collection of wise sayings that Solomon is passing on to his sons. Wise sayings are generally true, but not without exception. For example, in chapter 22 alone there are at least five other statements of probability. Look at verses 4, 11, 14, 16, and 26. Each is a statement that could sound like a guarantee, but none is. Rather, each is meant to reveal the wisdom of living righteously. For example, verse 4 states that *"Humility and the fear of the LORD bring wealth and honor and life."* Is that a guaranteed promise? Not at all – Jesus and his apostles were humble and God-fearing, yet they were poor, dishonored, and suffered greatly.[11] But as

---

[11] 1 Cor 4:9-13

a general rule, it is a true statement – a man who lives humbly and fearing the Lord, has the character and clarity of mind to be successful in business and in society.

Proverbs 22:6 simply says that diligent training will bear lasting fruit in our children's lives. They may follow Christ unwaveringly from childhood into old age, or they may reach adulthood like the prodigal son and make wrong choices for a season before repenting. It is also possible that they may stay at home submissively like the prodigal's older brother, yet inside be a prodigal with a heart full of self-righteousness and bitterness. (This particular scenario is less embarrassing for a parent, but still reveals the potential for sinful choices in an adult child.) In all honesty, it is also a remote possibility that a prodigal may stay in rebellion and never return to Christ.

In Proverbs 22:6 we receive encouragement towards diligent training of our children, but we must remember that they are neither animals to be dominated nor mindless plants to be pruned and bound. They are self-determining individuals who are processing their upbringing and will one day have their own time of reckoning with God.

Unfortunately, too many parents assume that the "training" in Proverbs 22:6 refers to intense control of their young adult children; so to prevent their teens from going prodigal they tightly restrict and dominate them. They fail to notice the tone in which Solomon shared the Proverbs with his teenage sons -- he never once threatened them with punitive consequences as their father. He came along side of them as fellow adults and warned them of reaping natural consequences for poor choices. Solomon modeled for us how to influence through love and respect.[12]

I wish Bev and I had understood this when our oldest three were young. We saw them as wet clay that would succumb to our persistent shaping, so we not only *taught* them, but also dominated and controlled them well into their teens. We were chiefly authoritarian in our approach, and rarely saw our children respond to us with disrespect. We weren't ogres – our home was full of affection – but we relied upon fear of consequence as the main source of

---

[12] For a more exhaustive discussion of Solomon's approach to parenting teens, listen to my series Parenting Teens With the Wisdom of Solomon. It contains everything I wish I had understood when my oldest children were teenagers.

motivation for our children. What we didn't realize was that there is a great difference between *intimidating children into subjection* and *winning their hearts into submission*. Intimidating children into subjection merely gains outward compliance. Having their hearts means gaining greater opportunity to influence their values.

Lest someone misunderstand me, let me emphasize that I still believe what I wrote in my Child Training Tips book, and regard firm control of our children in their younger years as critical for the maturing process. Establishing strong parental control early on in life is necessary, because as our young children learn to submit to *outer* controls they concurrently develop *inner* controls. And young children who are trained to have inner controls (self-control) are more receptive to values taught them as they grow. However, as our children head into adolescence, if we find ourselves still focused on influencing them chiefly through tight control and threat of consequence, we shouldn't be surprised if they begin to manifest an independent spirit some time during their teen years.

I have observed too many "obedient" model homeschoolers, who left their families and/or abandoned their parents' values sometime after their 18th birthday. Mind you, many of these parents ran such a tight ship that they were absolutely certain that their kids would continue to be obedient and godly into their adult years. And many of these parents were admired for their well-behaved teenage children. There is a great temptation for such a parent to develop a false security in his or her ability to control. Needless to say, when good children grow up and abandon the values of those with that perspective, it has a way of bringing their parents humility -- at least *it should*.

One indication that we tend toward overdependence on control is that we always want to know what we can **do** to achieve desired results with our kids. Of course, such a statement will confuse some because they are reading this book to find out what they are **to do**. So let me tell you a story about Pastor Richard Wurmbrand, the Romanian pastor who was imprisoned and tortured for 14 years by the communists – a truly seasoned saint.

On the evening of Easter Sunday in 1988 Pastor Wurmbrand was speaking to our newly planted church when it was meeting in our home. He finished what he wanted to say to us and opened the floor for questions. My wife

Beverly was first to speak and asked him what we could do as a new church to grow, be healthy, and advance the kingdom. His response took us off guard – he said, *"I do not have the answer to that question. Who has the next question?"* He then took a question from a young man, a political activist, who wanted to know what we could do in America to prevent the same kind of persecution the church endured in Romania. In response, Pastor Wurmbrand said, *"I cannot answer this question either. And now I want to tell you why. I cannot answer your questions because they are the wrong questions. To ask, 'What must I do...?' is like asking 'What is the melody of a prune?' A prune has no melody. As Christians we cannot ask 'What must I do...?' We must ask <u>'What must I be...?'</u>"*

His point was that fruitful Christianity comes from the inside out – from *who* we are – not from *what* we do. It is the inside that must first be changed, and then the heart will give birth to healthy, genuine expressions. For example, a shortsighted question asks, "What can I do to *show* love to my lesbian sister?" Would it not be better to actually *love* her? The first approach is concerned with outside appearances – the second is based on what is actually in the heart, and will have far greater impact. At issue is not the *appearance* of love, but actually *having* it. With our children, when we preoccupy ourselves with what to **do** -- with following all the right steps and enforcing all the standards given us by homeschool veterans – we will merely be controlling the outside. It is as though we have nothing genuine to pass on at a heart level, so we do what we can from the outside in.

For many years I presented a convention workshop entitled "Creating a Strong Family Identity." It was popular as a keynote address and generated great response from audiences. It contained various steps that parents could follow to strengthen family bonds. It was a good session, but it did not go deep enough. I created that session from observing families with strong family identities, but I eventually came to realize that their bonds did not entirely result from the steps I had documented. Their strong family connections were actually forged by their *love* for each other – not from the path they were on. The steps merely added to the bond created by the love. Many of those who listened to my suggested steps went home and implemented them, and I have heard back from many who were pleased with the results. However, significant family bonds are created not by external controls and steps along a path, but are a fruit of love in a home. Our goal should chiefly be the cultivation of Christ's love – first in our own hearts[13] and then in our families.

I once read an article written by a veteran homeschooler on how to raise children with a kingdom-minded worldview. The author had seen her own children grow up to be active in outreach, so offered readers the many steps she and her husband had developed to cultivate a vision for outreach in their children. I appreciated the value of the suggestions offered in the article – they were truly inspiring. However, I am convinced that their own children grew up with a vision for outreach – not because they as parents did all the steps, but because they as Christians genuinely owned the vision and it was contagious to their children. It was not what they *did* – it was *who* they were. The steps she offered in her article she did not learn at a conference and then impose upon her children. They were simply expressions of what was already in the hearts of she and her husband. After reading the article I pictured multitudes

---

[13] Eph 3:17-19

of moms implementing all the steps in the process, thinking that that is what it would take to raise kingdom-minded children. I fear that many of those moms, even if they can implement all those steps in their homes, will be in for a rude awakening when their children reach their older teen years. Our children spiritually blossom, not from the controls we impose from the outside, but from what they catch from us on the inside. (More on this point in a future book.)

Returning to my original point, parents who want to influence their children during the teen years must not rely strictly upon their authority to keep their children obedient. Solomon set for us a great example of balanced parenting – he admonished his young adult children and gave them commandments,[14] but he knew that for them to honor his commands he needed their hearts. That's why he said, *"My son, give me your heart and let your eyes keep to my ways"* (Prov 23:26). Solomon obviously didn't think he had the wisdom to "win" their hearts or the power to manipulate them. He

---

[14] *Prov 6:20 My son, observe the commandment of your father, And do not forsake the teaching of your mother (Also: Prov 3:1; 4:1-4)*

therefore appealed to his sons to make a decision to entrust their hearts to him.

I find it interesting that the apostle Paul dealt in a similar manner with New Testament believers. He knew how much he needed the hearts of those he exhorted, and therefore told them *"... although in Christ I could be bold and order you to do what you ought to do, yet I appeal to you on the basis of love..."* (Philemon 1:8-9). If we are to have significant influence on our teenage children we must have their hearts. Having their hearts means gaining the opportunity to influence *who they are,* not just *what they do.*

Blind Spot #6
Over-Reliance Upon Sheltering

An over-dependence on control in a family is often accompanied by an over-reliance on sheltering of children. It is not uncommon for homeschool parents to feel that since they filter whatever their children see and hear, they will control the results in their lives. That was *me* for many years. I remember saying to people, *"I am controlling the influences in my children's lives, so I am going to control the outcome."* I was absolutely certain that my children would be exempted from significant temptation and from developing particular bad habits because I was controlling what touched their lives.

I took nothing for granted and evaluated the effects of everything that had contact with my family. I got rid of the TV antennae when my older children were little and allowed them to watch only approved videos, ie: ones with no boy/girl relationships or occult powers -- Popeye and Mary Poppins were therefore out. They would attend birthday parties for children from church, but I would instruct them that if the birthday boy or girl's mother tried to show a video on my "no-watch" list, they were to go to a back bedroom and entertain themselves until the video was over. We carefully screened the music they heard and watched them cautiously when they were with friends.

My children could not play with most children in the neighborhood and were even kept away from some children in "like-minded" families. They were sheltered from secular publications, let alone any Christian books or magazines that promoted values that didn't match my own. Youth groups or Scouting were unheard of. Santa Claus, Halloween, and Harvest parties, as well as Superheroes and Barbie's, were anathema. I hardly wanted them to go into Wal-Mart or grocery stores lest they be exposed to images of immodestly dressed women. If the family's driving route was going to take us past a striptease club I would sternly admonish my sons to not even look slightly in the direction of the building. My standards were not as radical as others' I have known, but I was extremely selective about what my family was exposed to. I wanted to be absolutely certain my children were protected from any corrupting influences. Little did I know that it would take a lot more than my great emphasis on sheltering to achieve the results I desired.

In the last five years I have heard countless reports of highly sheltered homeschool children who grew up and abandoned their parents' values. Some of these children were never allowed out of their parents' sight and were not permitted to be in any kind of group setting, even with other "like-minded" kids, yet they still managed to develop an appetite for the world's pleasures. While I've seen sheltered children grow up and turn away from their parents' standards, conversely, I've known some Christian young people who went to public school, watched TV, attended youth groups, and dated, yet they walk in purity, have respectful, loving relationships with their parents, and now enjoy good marriages. Their parents broke all the "rules of sheltering," yet these kids grew up close to their families and resilient in their walks with Christ. Super-strict sheltering was obviously not the ultimate answer for them.

Protecting from temptations and corrupting influences is part of raising children. Every parent shelters to one degree or another. We all set standards for diet, for relationships, for reading and entertainment.

One permits the children to watch network television, but prohibits cable movie stations; another forbids network TV, but allows parent-approved videos; still another tolerates only parent-approved *Christian* videos; and another permits only books. All parents shelter – they just draw their lines in different places.

Protecting our children is not only a natural response of paternal love, but fulfills the commands of God. The Scriptures are clear that we are to make no provision for our flesh[15] and are to avoid all corrupting influences.[16] It warns us that bad company corrupts good morals[17] and that those who spend too much time with bad people may learn their ways[18] and suffer for it.[19] Just as our Father in heaven will not allow us to be tempted beyond what we can bear,[20] we rightly keep our children out of situations they will lack the moral strength to handle. Young children are weak and we are to protect the weak.[21]

---

[15] Rom 13:14
[16] 2 Cor 6:17-7:1
[17] 1 Cor 15:33
[18] Prov 22:24-25
[19] Prov 13:20
[20] 1 Cor 10:13
[21] 1 Thes 5:12

God understood the vulnerability of human nature when he gave the Israelites instructions before they entered the Promised Land. He told them to chase out the idol-worshipping Pagans in the land, lest His people associate with them and be drawn into idolatry.[22] The Israelites disregarded God's protective warning and allowed some Pagans to remain in the land. Consequently, each successive generation of young people was lost to idolatry. God instructed them to shelter their families, but their neglect of His warnings brought pain to their children and to their grandchildren for many generations.

Sheltering our families from bad influences is critical for their safety, but it is possible to become imbalanced and rely too heavily upon sheltering. We do this in a couple of ways.

1. We are imbalanced when *sheltering from harm* is the predominant expression of our parenting. Are we more concerned with *protecting our kids from that which is bad* or with *putting **into** them that which is good*? I want to ask that again: Are we more concerned with *protecting our kids from that which is bad* or with *putting **into** them that which is good*? Consider

---

[22] Ex 23:32-33; Num 33:51-56; Josh 23:7-13

that rearing children is like creating a family menu. If we keep them away from all junk food and feed them only prunes, their bodies will respond negatively. Protection from too much junk food is obviously a good idea, but their bodies need balanced nutrition. Physical health is achieved by both avoiding what is harmful and taking in a balance of what is good. To raise spiritually and morally healthy children we need to do the same. We must certainly protect them from harmful influences, but *more* than that, we must give them that which strengthens them spiritually and morally.

In my case I protected my oldest children from *harm* more than I invested into them *health*. I certainly taught my children a great deal about God and Kingdom living – we saturated them with the Word and Kingdom stories. Their lives were full of outreach and ministry, but comparatively, I was most intense about sheltering. I was continually analyzing the effects of every aspect of life, and my children never knew what thing Dad would declare off-limits next. Those parents who aren't analyzers like me just wait for their favorite teacher to expose for them the next unseen danger to their family. In imbalanced homes parents are <u>most</u> passionate about protecting children from harmful influences, and the children see that passion, then come to view Christianity as mostly about "avoiding bad stuff." When protection from the world becomes ***the defining characteristic of Christianity***, we shouldn't be surprised if our kids grow up and forsake the lifeless "religion of avoidance" they learned from us. As I stated in Chapter 4, that is not a faith most children are drawn to; in fact, it is one that will likely repel them.[23]

Please note that the operative word in my assessment is *passion*. Our children learn what's important to us not by what we verbally emphasize, but by what they see us *passionate* about. It is the intensity of our reaction to potential corruption that elevates to our children our priorities. If they see a greater intensity in us for their *sheltering* than they do for their *equipping*, we shouldn't be surprised if they come to view Christianity negatively as a "religion of avoidance." (In fact, our intensity may actually create a mystique and raise curiosity toward that which is forbidden.)

---

[23] For further discussion on this topic I refer you to my book, Child Training Tips

Let's ask ourselves, if the kids hear Uncle Bill say a swear word at the family reunion, do they see us "freak out," yet in contrast, whenever we are offended do they see us allow ourselves to hold the offense a long time? If they happen to look at an immodestly dressed woman on a magazine cover at the store, do we "lose it" and lecture them, yet in contrast, do they see us, without repentance, grumble against those who are over us in the Lord? The intensity of our emotions on an issue is what impacts our children most. In fact, I once heard it said that our children learn what is important not from what we say, but from what they see us "stress out" over.

Yes, it is right to value and protect our children's moral innocence, and it is natural for us to react with intensity to anyone or anything that might rob them of that innocence. However, when we treat every minor issue as a threat deserving of our outrage, it is possible we are defining Christianity for our children in a negative way.

After watching multitudes of highly sheltered children grow up and chase after the very things from which their parents sought to keep them, and seeing less-sheltered children grow up and walk strong, I am more selective about which hill I want to die on. I now pick my battles more carefully. I have concluded that fruitful parenting is more about what we put into our children than what we protect them from.

2. Sheltering is a critical part of parenting, but if parents keep it their primary focus, the children will grow up ill equipped to handle the temptations in the world.

When we enter the world as infants we arrive with immune systems still in development. Because we have had no contact with germs or disease while in the womb, our bodies need to come in contact with them, so that we can develop immunities. Babies who are isolated and kept in germfree environments fail to develop sufficient resistance, so succumb more easily to diseases when they grow older and encounter them. Medical inoculations only succeed because God has designed the body with the capacity to develop antibodies against disease. A child isolated from disease may appear to be of the greatest health to his parents, but the health of the human body is only proven by how it withstands an attack. A weak constitution succumbs to every germ and virus – a strong one fights them off. Our spiritual and moral health is developed and proved in the same way.

If we isolate our kids from the world until they are adults they may appear to us to be spiritually minded and strong in character. However, it is how they ultimately engage the world that proves their spiritual resilience. This is because sheltering does not *transform* the human heart – it merely *preserves* it, temporarily. Sheltering is nothing more than keeping something flammable away from a fire.

It is true that a boxer trains without an opponent until his coach decides he is ready for an actual fight. And it is true that a farmer might raise plants in a greenhouse until they are mature enough to be transplanted and face the various elements of nature. So also, we keep our children away from bad influences when they are young and need to grow unhindered in character and spiritual wisdom. The problem is that sheltering without significant preparation to engage the world fails to equip them. In fact, it may insure that they will fall in their first solo encounters.

Growing up isolated from temptation can develop a child who appears spiritually strong, but the appearance is not reality. When I was in college in 1974 I moved to northern California to live for a summer in a Christian commune. I was somewhat isolated from the world and surrounded by an amazing support system of my fellow "Jesus people." I remember feeling so full of faith, so committed to holiness, and so in love with God that summer. However, the "spirituality" I felt and the level of holiness I achieved was not real and could not endure testing. At the end of summer I returned to college in Southern California and discovered that I had not developed true spiritual muscles – when faced with temptation I fell flat on my face every time. The communal environment, isolated from significant temptation, had not prepared me for the battle I would face in the world. Valid spiritual growth required that *I face temptation* and *develop the capacity to resist it*, which eventually I did. My isolation from temptation had left me like a boxer who had shadow boxed, trained rigorously, and looked good in his trunks, but had never faced a sparring partner, let alone a true opponent.

Many sincere Christians return from retreats and church camps the same way. Over several days they are isolated from the world, surrounded with fellowship, and saturated with the Word of God. They come home feeling deeply spiritual. However, within a few days after returning they discover their "mountain top high" has faded away. So also, the spirituality our sheltered children achieve may only be spiritual fluff. If we want to prepare them to thrive in the world we must take them into it and teach them how to engage it. As part of that preparation I have several recommendations:

a. <u>Take time to teach them about God and living in His kingdom</u>. I emphasize this particularly for dads who are careful to shelter, but rarely get around to actually instructing their children in the faith. Too many fathers are quick to forbid all TV and youth groups, but never take the time to sit down and acquaint their children with the Word and how it points us to God. Preparing children to face the world requires more than keeping them away from its corruptions – parents must put into them Truth that will draw them to God. It is those children who have found God irresistible who will be faithful to Him.

True Christianity is not merely a system of religious beliefs that can be embraced or forsaken – it is a relationship between individuals and God. Therefore, Christians are not strengthened simply by massive doses of indoctrination. Our faith is strengthened as we discover God in the Word, and as we walk with Him we find Him to be trustworthy. If we want our children to remain faithful to God we must do all we can to lead them to Him, not just to a "system of faith."

Keep in mind that Bible instruction by itself is not some magic ingredient in a "parenting formula." Many homeschool prodigals were heavily groomed in the Scriptures. We do best when we faithfully use the Scriptures to reveal to children the Lord *Himself*. Remember Jesus' words in John 5:39, *"You diligently study the Scriptures because you think that by them you possess eternal life. These are the Scriptures that testify about me."* It is faith in *Christ* that carries us – not faith in *Christianity*.

b. <u>Pass on a pure faith.</u> It has been said that faith is *caught* and not *taught*, and I would agree. I have seen more than a few young married people who grew up in the public schools, but who walked in purity and close to Christ through their teen years, and are still close to their parents. What their parents gave them was not the gift of extreme sheltering, but the gift of a sincere faith in Christ. Homeschool parents must give the same gift to their children.[24] The problem is that we cannot give what we do not have. If we want to give our children a lasting and sincere faith in Christ, then we must first have it ourselves.

What is the faith in us that our children see? Is it what I discussed in the first six chapters -- a faith degraded by our missteps in parenting? Allow me to recap those first six points:

1. If the dreams we have for our children are really about *us*, might not they feel undue pressure to make *us* a success? In other words, is the faith they see in us a self-centered one?

2. If we have regarded them as a trophy, do they feel our intensity about not making the family look bad in public? In other words, is the simplicity of our faith polluted by our pride?

3. If we have emphasized outward form to our children, might not they equate holiness

---

[24] 1 Tim 1:5; 2 Tim 1:5

with external appearances? In other words, has the grace of our relationship with Christ been slowly traded for a phariseeistic concern for externals?

4. If they hear us pronounce judgments of others, might they not learn from us self-righteousness or fear of judgment? In other words, is it possible they see in us a faith that is both shallow and proud?

5. If our homes are controlled chiefly by intimidation and fear, might not our children feel like they are inconsequential, non-persons? In other words, are we losing the very relationship with our teens we need to attract them to our Lord?

6. If we over-elevate sheltering as an ingredient in our parenting formula, is it possible our children might come to believe that Christianity is mostly about avoiding bad stuff? In other words, although our Lord never told people to shelter themselves from anything except self-righteous, judgmental, religious leaders, do we present an inaccurate (and unattractive) picture of him?

The apostle Paul told the Galatian church that he was concerned for their faith. They had started off with a simple faith in Christ, but had polluted it by seeking to make themselves acceptable to God, with what they did or didn't do: *"Are you so foolish? After beginning with the Spirit, are you now trying to attain your goal by human effort?"* (Gal 3:3). In the same way, we may have started off years ago with a simple, undefiled faith, but the more we got caught up in all the "works" of intense parenting, the more we moved away from a simple faith contagious to our children. It is critical for our sake, let alone for our children, that we enjoy a life-giving faith in Christ with no religious trappings added to it. I don't believe that I can adequately explain this concept in a few paragraphs, so please be encouraged that I will be addressing it in detail in a future book.

c. Expose them to the world a little at a time, so that they will not be overwhelmed by its attraction when they finally face it. Just as babies raised in germfree environments more easily contract diseases, so also do Christians who have not encountered the world.

After the Iron Curtain fell in the Soviet Union, our church developed a ministry to help Russian and Ukrainian immigrants assimilate into the U.S. Over the years my wife and I got to know many immigrant families and we marveled at what it was like to raise a family under Communism. Back in the Soviet Union homeschooling and private Christian schools had not been legal, and parents were forced to send their children to Communist schools where one of the instructors' goals was to indoctrinate the students in atheism. From the testimonies we heard, parents equipped their children at home and the children's faith typically remained intact.

It was our observation however, that within a year after being in the U.S. these same children started to go morally astray. They were like the proverbial germfree baby, since in the Soviet Union they had never encountered the level of moral corruption found here. They had developed no resistance to temptation and were not morally prepared to handle American entertainment, vulgar playmates, and values of "tolerance" at school. Soviet parents, who had prepared their children to handle the pressures of godless atheism, had lacked the opportunity to equip their children to handle moral pressures. They found themselves here in America thrilled with their new freedom, but distressed by the way Americans exercised their liberty.

When my youngest son was 8 years old, he asked me why we took him into Wal-Mart when we shopped. He was distressed because he found himself noticing women's underwear advertisements hanging around the store. I acknowledged his distress and encouraged him to pray for the models, that they would value modesty and come to faith in Christ. Knowing he would face harder tests in life than Wal-Mart ads, I wanted him, by occasional exposure, to become desensitized to such images, and I wanted him to develop a wholesome, prayerful response to those who tempt him.

In a society like ours, so full of immodest fashions, desensitization eventually will happen, but our children's greatest need is to have compassion for those who tempt them. The root of lust is self-centeredness, so the more selfless and loving our children are, the less they will be impacted by lust. I therefore encourage parents to concentrate on raising children who selflessly love others. I have found that praying for those who tempt us accomplishes two things – the recipient receives prayer and we see them through the eyes of God. Those who see others from God's perspective will tend to have compassion on them as lost souls.[25]

d. <u>Take them into the world on the *offense*, not *defense*</u>. A major reason many parents choose to homeschool their children is that they are concerned about negative socialization in the classroom setting. They want control over *when* and *how* their children are faced with outside influences. When the children are confronted by the world the parents want to be there as guides. I understand this perspective, but such a view is inadequate. I want to be with my children when they encounter the world, but not merely so that they will survive it. Survival has to do with self-preservation, and is concerned with self, not others. Like a good captain I want to be with my children, so that I can lead them

---

[25] Want help raising loving children? I suggest the CD set "Beyond Obedience: Raising Children Who Love God and Others." Also consider the study on 1 Corinthians 13 "The Power of Love."

offensively into battle. We and our children are warriors in God's kingdom, and we must take them into the world for the purpose of advancing that kingdom.

Jesus modeled this when he first called his disciples -- *"Follow me, and I will make you fishers of men."* Following Him did not mean hiding with Him in a monastery or remote community of likeminded believers, but going with Him into the world to seek and save the lost.[26] (Because his goal was to send his followers on a rescue mission into dangerous territory, he declared to his Father, *"My prayer is <u>not that you take them out of the world</u> but <u>that you protect them</u> from the evil one"* (John 17:15). Like Jesus, we must take our children into the world with a view to seeking and saving the lost. And his prayer for our safety while we do so continues to this day.

My youngest son played little league baseball every spring for many years, and I always helped out as an assistant coach. On occasion, when word of my son's involvement leaked out, I would be approached by a concerned homeschool

---

[26] Luke 19:10.

parent and questioned about the risks of such contact with unbelievers. They reminded me that my son would hear bad words, vulgar jokes, and bad attitudes – boys would even swear at him. I told them that that is exactly what I was anticipating.

I wanted my son to know how to respond when unkind people expressed themselves,[27] and I wanted to be with him when it happened. I wanted him to know he could survive quite well when others verbally abused him, but more importantly, I wanted to witness it so I can coach him through it. I especially wanted to be there so I could help him see the world through eyes of compassion – not fear. I believe that those homeschoolers, who don't just *survive* but *thrive* in the world, do so because they have a "kingdom" view of it. They see it as the place inhabited by the blind[28] who are potential members of God's kingdom.

A major problem for us may be that we do not *have* what we need to *give*. We lack a kingdom view, so cannot give it to our kids. The sheltering mindset common to some

---

[27] Luke 6:27-28
[28] 2 Cor 4:4

parents sometimes creates inward-focused families. We get so used to cutting ourselves off from everything that might threaten us that we end up separating ourselves not just from the world, but even from most Christians. God's goal for us is not that we raise strong family-minded children who grow up and meet other strong family-minded children, who then marry and raise more strong family-minded children, who grow up and do the same. That line of thinking is totally self-centered and renders God's people impotent as warriors for His kingdom. God's goal for all His warriors is to continually reach out to the lost in the world. That is why we are here.

When we lack this perspective we will run from those who need our gospel. As an example, let's say we are eating lunch with our family at McDonald's. During the meal the children notice a woman scrounging through the trashcans inside the restaurant looking for food scraps. How do we respond? When we notice her outfit is immodest by our standards, do we focus our children's attention elsewhere or gather them quickly and leave? Do we use her predicament as a teaching opportunity for our children, and explain that we can't give her any help since she is apparently too lazy to work? Or do we buy her some lunch and invite her to join us at our table? How our children see us respond to the lost will do more to influence them than all the books and stories we read to them.

I cannot spiritually impart a "kingdom view" to you, but *God* can. I therefore admonish all readers to beseech God that the eyes of their hearts be opened, that they would see the world through kingdom eyes.

e. <u>Cultivate a loving relationship with them</u>, which will allow you to speak into their lives and influence their values. I will deal with this issue at length later in another book, so suffice it to say that it is the key area of need I have discovered among my own and many other dedicated families. It has been my observation that in "control-oriented" homes, relationships between parents and teens are often weakest. For us to have influence over our teen's hearts, especially when they are engaging the world, our love relationships with them must be strong.

In the Bible we see that people obeyed God for two reasons – *fear* and *love*. King David sang of his love for God[29] and he also sang of the fear of God.[30] God wants His followers to be drawn to Him out of love,[31] and that's why it is His kindness that leads us to repentance.[32] But He also wants us to be kept on the path by fear of His authority.[33] That's why He told the Israelites He wanted both their *fear* and their *love; "And now, O Israel, what does the LORD your God ask of you but to fear the LORD your God, to walk in all his ways, to love Him, to serve the LORD your God with all your heart and with all your soul"* (Deut 10:12). With our children, it should be the same toward us.

If our children grow up motivated only by fear of consequence, they will eventually get away with what they can whenever we are not around.[34] If we have their hearts they will seek to honor us whether we are present or not, and their hearts will remain open to our influence. I refer you to the apostle Paul who modeled this approach to leadership perfectly, *"Therefore, although in Christ **I could be bold***

---

[29] Ps 18:1; 116:1; 119:159

[30] Ps 2:11; 22:25; 33:8

[31] Jer 31:3

[32] Rom 2:4

[33] Luke 12:5; 1 Pet 2:17

[34] Eph 6:6

***and order you** to do what you ought to do, 9 yet **I appeal to you on the basis of love**...*" (Phile 1:8-9a). Paul's pattern with the churches suggests he understood that *appeals* to love were more powerful than *commands* and *threats*. As an apostle, he could have issued personal commands many times, yet in his letters to the churches he *plead* with them 25 different times to do what was right, while he *personally commanded* them only twice.[35]

Many intense parents mistakenly think they have their children's hearts, and therefore do not seek to cultivate better relationships. Beverly and I were such parents. We were certain that because we shared so much affection with our children that we had their hearts. However, when we gave them instructions, it was never our children's love for us that we appealed to, it was their fear of our authority. This meant that our first three children were far more vulnerable to outside influences than they needed to be.

As intensely sheltered children grow into adolescence, and become aware of the different standards between families, some

---

[35] 2 Th 3:6,12

are attracted to others' standards. They do not understand why the clothes you forbid them to wear, are worn by other Christians. They may not be able to grasp why you do not allow movies that many of their friends are permitted to see. If your relationship with your children is strong and based in love, they will honor your standards, and try to grasp your reasoning. But if their heart connection to you is weak, they will care little of your reasoning and look more to their friends for relationship and identity.

f. <u>Help them find security in their relationship with you</u>. When my oldest son was almost 16 we let him get his first job washing dishes at a restaurant managed by a Christian friend of ours. As diehard shelterers we wrestled with whether or not our son was ready to enter the world's workforce. We knew we couldn't shelter him forever, and so finally concluded that he should be old enough to send into the world two nights a week. What we didn't realize was that he would be working with drug-using, tattooed, partiers, and our Christian friend was never scheduled to work our son's shift.

Within a month it became apparent that our son's new work associates were having an effect on him. He came home one evening and asked, *"Dad, can I dye my hair blue?"* After my wife was finally able to peel me off the ceiling, I laid into him, reminding him whose son he was, and that I would not have people at church telling their children not to be like the pastor's son. I explained that just because he wanted to use washable dye, it didn't make me any happier. (Note that my intense reaction had to do with "outward appearances" and the impact on me.)

Of course, my wife and I immediately began to evaluate whether we had made a mistake by letting him take the job. After an intense discussion we decided to coach him more carefully and let him keep his job.

Two months later he came home from work and asked me if he could pierce his ear. Again, my wife had to peel me off the ceiling. He thought it might be okay since he wanted a *cross* earring – like I was supposed to be happy, because it would be a "sanctified" piercing. If that wasn't enough, he also wanted to get a tattoo! But it was going to be okay, because it would be a Christian tattoo!

Needless to say, my mind was absolutely blown! I thought I had raised him better than this. I imaged that some day we might deal with a questionable haircut or some unacceptable music, but I would never have guessed that his values could change so quickly or so severely. What took me over the edge was not just that he suddenly had outrageous values, but that he thought I might go along with him! It immediately became obvious that he was not ready to handle the world. To our relief, he volunteered to quit the job.

One day, several years later, I was looking back and evaluating our approach to sheltering. Something my son said shortly after he started his job kept coming back to me. When I picked him up the second night of work, he got in the car with a big smile on his face and said *"They like me!"* As I dwelt on that comment, it suddenly came clear to me – my son had finally met someone who liked him for who he was. Few others in his entire life had shown him much acceptance, especially not his mother and I. It is no exaggeration – in our efforts to shape and improve him, all we did was find fault with everything he did. We loved him dearly, but he constantly heard from us that what he did (who he was) wasn't good enough. He craved our approval, but we couldn't be pleased. Years later, I realized he had given up trying to please us when he was 14, and from then on he was just patronizing us.

The reason our son wanted to adorn himself like his work associates, was because they accepted him for who he was. He wanted to fit in with those who made him feel significant. He wanted to be like those who gave him a sense of identity. The problem wasn't one that could be solved by extended sheltering – he could have been sheltered until he was 30 and he still would have been vulnerable. The problem was that we had sent our son into the world insecure in who he was. He went into the world with a hole in his heart that is best filled by his parents and by God.

I have since observed that what best equips children to handle the pressures of the world is security in who they are. Whether believer or unbeliever, those young people who are least tempted to follow the crowd are those who are secure in themselves and don't need the approval of others. The Bible calls insecurity the *fear of man* – it is allowing other's opinions of us to affect our values and choices. At the very least, if we want to prepare our children to stand tall in the world we need to help them find security in their relationship with us, and more importantly, with God.

In a future book I will share how we can participate with God to help our children find security. Those who don't want to wait for the book can order the CD set "Influencing Children's Hearts."[36]

I believe that a primary reason we can over-rely on sheltering is because it is the easiest part of parenting to do. It requires no planning, little preparation, or expenditure of energy. It takes minimal immediate brainpower. We simply assess something might be harmful and say to our children, "NO." It's an aspect of parenting that is effortless to do, yet seems to promise an extreme impact. I don't know if I would go so far as to call it *lazy* parenting, but I will say that investing into our children does take a lot more work and much more time.

Before we leave this topic, we must consider the possibility that we are drawn to over-

---

[36] 800-545-1729

dependence on sheltering because it appeals to the Pharisee in us. Maintaining a righteous appearance and avoiding uncleanness characterized the most religious people of Christ's day, and he didn't tolerate it.[37] Avoiding anything that seemed to defile made them feel "holy" and it does the same for us. The more we fixate on keeping our families away from corruption the prouder we can become of our higher standards. It may even get to the place that we can't wait for opportunities to boast or "share" with others the standards we hold, ie: an invitation for our children to watch a movie, attend a Bible club, or accept a questionable gift, etc.). Pride is a dangerous sin because it blinds us to itself – it is the filter through which we see. *Spiritual* pride is even more dangerous because it involves what we think is righteousness.[38] May God open our eyes that we might see why we are so prone to imbalance in this area.

Since you died with Christ to the basic principles of this world, why, as though you still belonged to it, do you submit to its rules: 21 "Do not handle! Do not taste! Do not touch!"? 22 These

---

[37] Luke 7:39-47; 15:2; Mark 7:15; Mat 15:17-20
[38] Luke 18:11-12

are all destined to perish with use, because they are based on human commands and teachings. 23 Such regulations indeed have an appearance of wisdom, with their self-imposed worship, their false humility and their harsh treatment of the body, but they lack any value in restraining sensual indulgence. Col 2:20-23

Lest this chapter be taken wrong, and some readers misinterpret my intentions, I want to emphasize that I am still a strong proponent of sheltering our children. My goal has been to alert parents to the problem of *over-reliance* on sheltering. If you have finished this chapter, and are under the impression that I no longer believe in it, I would encourage you to go back and reread it.

Blind Spot #7
Formulaic Parenting Hinders Relationship

An over-dependence on authority and control, along with an over-reliance upon sheltering are often part of a "formulaic" approach to parenting. We, as homeschool parents, are committed to achieving results with our children so we look for and rely upon formulas and self-working principles to insure our success. One of the reasons we go to homeschool conventions and read numerous books is to learn the guaranteed "how to's" and steps from the successful veterans. Our desire for results with our family compels us to discover all the ingredients in the ultimate "family-life recipe."

Formulas for success after all, have become the American way – impatience and love of expedience characterize our outlook on life. That is why millions of self-help books are sold every year in bookstores, both secular and Christian. By its very definition, a formula is a reliable process of producing a specified result. In life, we want the ultimate formula for weight loss, the quickest scheme to get rich, and the surefire prescription for finding true love. In the church we want the proven method for church growth, the sure techniques for evangelism, and the most effective system for raising up leaders. And with our children we want the tried and true approach for producing results. The process doesn't need to be quick or simple, but it must be reliable, and it certainly must be *biblical*. To our delight, we know the Bible is full of the wisdom and promises of God. We therefore look to it for its self-working principles and promised methods.

Yes, it seems that everyone in the church these days wants to find the biblical formulas for success, but there's a problem with trusting in formulas – we are directed, no, *commanded* to trust in **God** – not in formulas.[39] There is a monumental difference.

A formulaic perspective says, *"If I am faithful to implement this principle or carry out this procedure properly, I am certain to arrive at a specific result. And If I do not do the procedure exactly right I will achieve bad results."* In this state of mind we are trusting not just in the "method," but also in **our efforts** to carry it out. *Trust in formulas is really dependence upon*

---

[39] John 14:1; Ps 37:5; 62:8

ourselves. In our hearts we know this and that's why those who feel their efforts have produced great results are tempted to take pride in their adult children – they credit themselves for doing it all right (and condescend to those who haven't). And that's why those unhappy with the results of their efforts feel so much like failures – they conclude they must have used the wrong approach.

I have heard from too many parents who feel like failures, and they are especially baffled as they list all that they did or didn't do: *no TV, no videos, no video games, no dating, no bad music, no youth group, no institutional church, no neighborhood friends; they homeschooled, dressed modestly, groomed conservatively, memorized the Scriptures, and baked their own bread.* They were intensely dedicated to rearing their children for God, but their trust was not really in God alone – it was in what they did for God.

I have also seen parents who take great pride in how their adult children turned out, and they are more than willing to tell others the steps they took to get them that way: *no TV, no videos, no video games, no dating, no bad music, no youth group, no institutional church, no neighborhood friends; they homeschooled, dressed modestly, groomed conservatively, memorized the Scriptures, and baked their own bread.* Hmmmm...

Anyone who really understands the grace of the gospel knows that we cannot take personal credit for any spiritual accomplishments. We are totally God's workmanship[40] and everything good in our lives is a gift from Him.[41] We can do absolutely nothing by ourselves for which we can take credit.[42] Yes, when we face God on Judgment Day he will affirm us for what we have done here on Earth,[43] but we know He is the power behind our lives,[44] so we rightly give all glory to Him.[45] So many of us lean toward a formulaic mentality, because our fallen natures are drawn toward *self-reliance.* We want to feel that by our own efforts (works) we have achieved something that will make us acceptable to God – by nature we are legalistic. (The reason that "human effort" forms the basis for all false religions of the world is because our fallen natures strive toward "high self-esteem" through

---

[40] Eph 2:10; Phil 2:13; 1:6
[41] James 1:17
[42] Eph 2:8-9; Gal 6:14; Rom 4:2; 1 Cor 1:28-31; 2 Cor 11:30
[43] 1 Cor 3:6-15; Mat 25:21
[44] Acts 17:28
[45] Rom 11:36

self-effort. In contrast, **grace** gives credit to God for all that is good and deprives us of any kind of self-credit.)

It is critical to understand that God wants us to trust not in principles, methods, or formulas, no matter how "biblical" they seem. God wants us to trust in HIM! As I emphasized earlier on in this book, our responsibility is to **obey** – God's job is to produce results.[46] Our success in raising children to be lovers of God and others, is not going to be contingent upon achieving perfect sheltering or using the best Bible curriculum. It is going to be based on doing what we must as parents, but trusting *God* for the outcome. We absolutely mustn't trust in our ability to intimidate and control, or in the "path" upon which we lead our family.

If Christians can consistently achieve seemingly spiritual results by human efforts, I ask – where is God in the equation? After studying how God dealt with Israel and how Christ conducted Himself on Earth, I contend that God will not reduce Himself to being an ingredient in a formula or method. Please consider, if a formula for success consistently produces results, where's God in the mix? For

---

[46] 1 Cor 3:6

example, if church growth can be consistently achieved by following one man's devised plan, yet only 10% of the members in a formula-grown church do 90% of the work, might not the low quality of the fruit suggest a problem with the method? And if a technique of evangelism consistently produces multiple "decisions" for Christ, yet 90% of souls "won" almost immediately fall away, is it possible the results are fleshly and not spiritual? In the church is it possible that we are trying to gain spiritual results by fleshly means? Yes, biblical principles of discipline, when used by believers or unbelievers, will help develop good behavior in children, but good behavior may only be skin-deep. Fruitful parenting is about affecting our children's *hearts*, not just their behavior. To influence their hearts, it won't be by our control – the heart belongs to the individual and must be touched by God.

I have observed that the best and most lasting fruit is born in families in which the gospel is genuinely believed and lived. Parents who daily depend upon God, and not their methods and self-working principles, are most likely to pass on their faith. I am convinced that the most contagious parenting is living a heartfelt faith before your children.

Children as people

There's a problem with approaching our relationships in a formulaic fashion. Can you guess what it is?

People, as self-willed individuals, cannot be successfully subjected to methods of manipulation. Our children are people – they are not soulless animals to be trained. Neither are they chemicals in a formula, which can be processed for guaranteed results. It is critical that we realize our children are people whose hearts, as they mature, are influenced more by relationship than by external controls. In all our intensity we can sometimes treat them not as fellow humans, but as dehumanized ingredients in a cake we are baking.

If we think we have total control over how our children respond to our training, we will relate to them not so much as people, but more as animals. Dogs are behavior-driven and can be trained to respond to a stimulus exactly the same way, time after time. Children however are people and as they mature they will eventually decide if they will continue to respond as trained. If we do not understand this we will fail to develop the relationship they deserve as our children, and as our younger brothers and sisters in Christ – which, incidentally, will give us greater influence over their adolescent hearts.

For years Bev and I studied the process of parenting. We read multitudes of books, watched hours of videos, and listened to many tapes. We wanted to do whatever it took to get results with our children. Nothing is wrong, of course, with growing in knowledge of biblical child training – in fact, it's good. However, we majored on the "process," and as we gleaned new techniques we would stir them into the parenting mix, subjecting our children to it. We did have great affection in our home, but we had the wrong idea of what it meant to have influential heart relationships. We loved our kids, but who they were as people was inconsequential to our process.

My own recipe called for great amounts of parental control, daily doses of Scripture indoctrination, plenty of edifying music, modest apparel, and safe entertainment, all combined in the oversized mixing bowl of sheltering, and cooked in the oven of homeschooling. The timer was set and I knew that when they reached their 18th birthday, "DING" the timer would go off I would have a perfect angel food kid. I was certain of it. I had yet to learn that fruitful parenting is more about *people* than *process*.

At homeschool conventions across the country I have seen in parents a tendency to treat children as non-persons. I cannot count the times I have stood at my booth in the exhibit hall and been approached by a mom or dad, accompanied by one of their older teenage children. The parents ask me about a problem they are having with one of their children, and as they talk, I realize that the child to whom they refer is the one standing there with them. It is as though these parents are oblivious that their young adult has feelings. As I look into the eyes of that embarrassed young person I often see a detached or despairing look that hints they can't wait to get out of the home. Other parents who approach me may not have a teen present to embarrass, but they will ask me for a method to change their problem-teenager at home. In the last few years I have tried to explain to these parents that fruitful interaction is not about *what they do* to their young people, but *who they are* with them. *It's about having a real faith in God, and expressing it in a real relationship with your children as real persons.*

Breakdown of relationship

A number of years ago, it finally dawned on Bev and I that as we had focused on parenting "methods," our children were eventually relegated to being ingredients in a formula. We related with them as if they were "projects." The more we focused on formulas and principles to which we would subject our children, the more they became "things." The more they became *things* the less we had significant *relationship*. The less we had *relationship* the more we lost their *hearts*. Without their *hearts* the less we were able to *influence them or their values*. We regularly spent hours coaching and admonishing them during their teen tears, not realizing that all our brilliant lectures were falling on deaf ears. Without their hearts, the best we could do was make more rules and devise new consequences, which affected the outside, but not the inside.

I want to restate the points of this last paragraph one at a time, so you can see the progression again:

1. The more we focus on formulas and principles, the more children become "things."

2. The more they become *things* the less we have significant *relationship*.

3. The less we have *relationship* the more we lose their *hearts*.

4. Without their *hearts* the less we are able to *influence their values*.

5. Without their hearts, the best we can do is control the outside (for a while).

Is it clear yet? I know that some reading this do not get it, because right now you are hoping I will lay out a step-by-step plan for winning your children's hearts. Ouch! The formulaic mentality, unfortunately, is like a filter that we wear over our eyes – it is a way of viewing the Christian life that must be identified and forsaken.

Perhaps it will become clearer if I illustrate the point using the husband-wife relationship.

Let's say that the situation involves a man and his wife. He goes off for a day to the ACME School for Husbands and returns home to put into practice all that he learns. Upon arising the first morning he pulls out a cue card, looks at his wife lying in bed and awkwardly reads, *"Honey... don't you look ..... beautiful today!"* She might be flattered, and does want to believe he is sincere, but she knows that with her mask of face cream she looks awful. Besides, although his words are nice, his need to *read* his "heart felt" love lines smacks of insincerity, and she doesn't trust his motives. Her hopes are up, after all, he is trying; but as the day progresses and he does one "good husband" deed after the other, it is obvious that he has merely learned some tricks for manipulating women. He cluelessly insults her cooking for the 17th time that month, then reaches into a box and pulls out a bouquet of plastic flowers to "fix it"; when his wife confronts him after he starts his daily tirade against his mother-in-law, he suddenly stops and begins reciting a contrived script about how wonderful his mother-in-law actually is; before responding to anything his wife says he first refers to a list of tips he carries in his pocket, etc.

Some women would be thrilled that their husband was at least trying, but most would prefer that he not simply *act* loving, but that he actually *love* them. A woman desires her husband not to *act* like he is listening to her, but to actually care enough to listen. She rightly desires a *real* relationship with her husband, and doesn't want to feel like she's another problem in his life to be dealt with. She wants *him* – not the cliché phrases or manipulative ploys he learned from an ACME instructor. Such a woman will not easily draw close to her husband – she may even be tempted to back away out of self-protection.

But what if a husband came home from the training and instead of trying to woo his wife, he treated her degradingly, seeking to coerce changes in her, ie: he threatened to take away all access to money if the house were not kept neater; he took away her car keys and cut off the phone to control how she spent her time; if she cried for any reason he would scream at her and accuse her of "classic female manipulation," etc. My guess is that most women would have great difficulty submitting to such demeaning treatment.

A woman's struggle with such harsh conduct is understandable, since as the Scriptures teach, a wife is to be sacrificially loved and tenderly cherished.[47] And she mustn't be treated roughly,[48] but regarded with special consideration and respect.[49] It is a foolish man who disregards God's shrewd admonishments – any wife with

---

[47] Eph 5:25, 28-29
[48] Col 3:19
[49] 1 Pet 3:7

self-respect will be tempted to keep herself at a safe emotional distance.

In these two scenarios the husband approached his wife with a formulaic mentality. He related to her like she was a project, subjecting her to various techniques and ploys to achieve a certain result. What he really needed to do was love his wife and relate to her genuinely on the basis of that love. In the same way that a wife needs to be esteemed as a woman and fellow adult, our children, particularly our teens, need to be respected. When we relate with them like they are *projects* they subconsciously see it in our eyes and sense it in our manner. They respond best to genuine interaction – respectful of them, as if they were intelligent beings with thoughts and opinions worth listening to. If we relate with them as if they are projects, rather than persons, they will likely remain emotionally distant from us. Yes, we are still responsible to protect them, exercise authority over them, and groom them toward full adulthood, but they must have opportunities to share their thoughts and know they have been heard. (I will address this with more specifics in a future book.)

It all goes back to my previous admonition – it is ***who*** you are not just ***what*** you do. A formulaic mentality is chiefly concerned with ***doing*** the right thing to produce the right result. Our children need us not merely to **act** like Christians, but to **be** genuine Christians. As I look back in my own life, I see that with my first three children I was too concerned with how they were perceived by others. I saw their behavior as a reflection on me, and I wanted to look good. They, therefore, sensed in me a measure of pretentiousness – not the genuineness of faith that would have drawn them to me or to the Jesus I spoke about. My sincere concern for their character was overshadowed by my concern for my reputation. I have discovered that, like me, multitudes of parents want their children's hearts, but live a faith that fails to completely attract them.

Influencing the heart

Formulaic parents typically tighten controls to insure a desired outcome, when what is really needed is to *increase their influence over their kids' hearts*. It is only reasonable that those who have the most power to influence our hearts are those to whom we are drawn. To whom are your children attracted? The cool kids at youth group? A celebrity? Their Uncle Bud? They are probably attracted to others for the same basic reasons we are:

1) We are drawn to those who succeed with our values. (That's what a *hero* is.)

2) We are drawn to those who can benefit us.

3) We are drawn to those who make us feel valuable. (We actually tend to adopt the values of those who like or respect us, especially if they have our respect.)

4) We are drawn to those who have earned our respect. (By showing they are someone to be reckoned with.)

5) We are drawn to fellow believers in whom Christ dwells with power.

If we want to influence our children's *hearts* and not just their *behavior*, it will happen because of *who* we are, not *what* we do. We cannot simply implement loving actions in our homes – we must truly love.[50] We cannot merely recite Scripture to our families – we must be those who look to the Word because it points to our wonderful Savior.[51] And we

---

[50] 1 Cor 13:3
[51] John 5:39

especially cannot treat a spiritual activity such as prayer as a "discipline" or "principle" – it must be the natural response of dearly loved children of God pouring their hearts out to their Father in Heaven.

Turning hearts of children to parents

God addresses the issue of having our children's hearts through one of the Minor Prophets. In the final verse of the Old Testament, God prophesies through Malachi that John the Baptist will not only come to prepare the way of the Lord, but *"He will turn the hearts of the fathers to their children, and the hearts of the children to their fathers..."* (Mal 4:6). So many family-minded people quote this passage, but I have rarely heard it exposited. Consider the following.

If Malachi 4:6 is a *true* prophesy, then when did John the Baptist fulfill it? In his preaching and teaching he never once mentioned *parents* or *children*, yet we know that because God spoke it, the prophetic word was true. It was even restated in Luke 1:17. Obviously, it was never God's intent that John directly address parent-child relationships. It is clear God meant that the hearts of parents and children be bonded as a **side effect** of John's ministry.

Of what, then, did John's ministry consist? John the Baptist preached the good news of the gospel,[52] calling people to repentance,[53] pointing to the Lamb of God[54] who would take away the sin of the world,[55] and reconcile people with God.[56] God intended that those who listened to John, and found reconciliation with God through Jesus, would be so changed that their families would be transformed as well. The gospel, if truly understood and embraced, will weave its binding fibers deep into the parent/child relationship. At the very least, it will make us *real* (genuine and honest, both with God and others).

It is possible that the pure gospel of Jesus, which first led us to Him, has become clouded for us. We may believe in the grace of the gospel, but we have unconsciously supplemented the finished work of Christ with our own efforts to implement our preferred formula. We may have muddied the gospel with our preoccupation with outward appearances and external controls.

---

[52] Luke 3:18
[53] Mark 1:4
[54] John 1:26,34,36
[55] John 1:29
[56] Luke 1:16

It could also be that we don't enjoy the fruit of the gospel in our families, because we have never understood the grace of the gospel at all. Either way, I pray that the eyes of our hearts be opened to see Jesus.[57] Those who see Him, most easily drop those things that hamper them in their pursuit of Him.[58] And those who *really* see Him find they more naturally become like Him.[59] And it is those who are genuinely like Him that have the greatest impact on those around them.

Seeing Jesus

Jesus was the greatest preacher of holiness the world has ever known, yet He attracted to Himself common sinners and the dregs of society. Jesus had high standards – He was the epitome of righteousness and purity, but somehow He was incredibly attractive. He exposed sin, but He accepted sinners. He hated evil, but evildoers saw in Him a wealth of mercy. Jewish society was intimidated by the standards of the Pharisees, but few were drawn to their religion of *avoidance, control,* and *form*. Is it possible that when our children look

---

[57] John 12:21; 20:29
[58] Heb 12:1-3
[59] 1 John 3:2

at us they see more of the Pharisees in us than Jesus? Might it be that the Jesus we represent to our children is not the real Jesus at all?

The best thing we can do to break away from a formulaic mentality and become a person of influence is to really grasp the grace of the gospel and live it out in our homes. For our children to see the beauty of the Savior in us we will need to find His beauty first. If we are not yet smitten with him, why do we think our children will be? We need to get to know the real Jesus.

Our Lord is wonderful and never meant that we live under the bondage of striving in our flesh to gain his pleasure. He never intended that the Christian life be one of oppression and heaviness. That's why He said to us, *"Take my yoke upon you and learn from me, for I am gentle and humble in heart, and you will find rest for your souls. For my yoke is easy and my burden is light"* (Mat 11:29-30). If we are not daily **enjoying the gentleness and humility of Jesus**, we are under a bondage He never meant for us. If we are not enjoying **His rest**, we are just like the Old Covenant Jews under the Law, laboring to please God by human efforts. Jesus said that following Him is **easy and not burdensome**. If our lives are not that – we are not following

Him. We have veered away into a life of doubt, drudgery, and uncertainty.

The Savior is near you and calls you to leave behind the life of empty, lifeless religion, and come to the One who embodies God's mercy. He is righteous – He abhors evil and despises pompous religion. He hates it exceedingly, but He loves us so much, He allowed Himself be nailed to a cross, so that the wrath of God would pour down upon *Him* instead of us. He now extends to us His scarred hands, so that we would see them and declare in our hearts, He is a wonderful Savior worth following!

Loving Him isn't about our children – it is about HIM! God intends that the side effect of loving Jesus, and enjoying the grace of the gospel, will be that all people, including our children, will be touched by the Savior in us. I pray in Jesus name that as you read these words you will experience the grace of God in a fresh and new way. Cry out for it! And may it rain down upon you with power from on high! May today be the day that you grasp the love of God and find in Him what you've been searching for all along.

AMEN!

More materials by Reb Bradley

Breaking Free: Escaping an Exclusive Christian Group – *book*

Influencing Children's Hearts – 4-CD set

Child Training Tips: *What I wish I knew when my children were young* – *book*

Biblical Insights into Child Training Establishing control in the home and raising godly children – 8 *CD/DVD set*

Parenting Teens With the Wisdom of Solomon: What the Bible Says About Raising Teenagers – *CD/DVD set*

The New Testament Home Church: *Its organization and structure* – *book*

Preparing Your Children for Courtship and Marriage: *From toddlers to teens.* 8-*CD/DVD set*

The Delightful Family – *How to create strong family bonds, raise joyful children, and minimize sibling rivalry* – 3 *CD set*

Powerful Christian Living: *Following Jesus into Wholeness.* Amazing series revealing Jesus' path to Christian maturity – *12 CD set*

Motives of the Heart: A biblical study in pride and humility *(very revealing)* – *3-CD or 6-DVD set*

Reconciling With Your Wife: Critical help for the husband who finds himself abandoned by his wife – *book*

For these materials or dozens of more titles, contact your source for this book, or request a complete catalog from
Family Ministries   800-545-1729
www.familyministries.com

Printed in Great Britain
by Amazon